Praise for

Track Tales

If you haven't shared the experiences of being close to racing folk, you should give yourself the opportunity to meet them, via the wonderful poems of a master storyteller and wordsmith. *Track Tales* is more than a collection of poems. It is a history book that chronicles a time in Australian life that will never be quite the same again.

~ John Holland, author of *Dry Bones*, *Under the Dog Star* and *Bitter Bread*

Reading *Track Tales* is like key-holing a personal diary that gives the human drum on the racing industry in Australia during the early 1980s. The poems perversely honour the men, women, horses and dogs that were the industry at the time ... the poems jostle at the starting gate. Suddenly they're off and running! A totally absorbing read.

~ Martin Christmas, author of *Immediate Reflections*

Mercedes Webb-Pullman illustrates her characters with a deft hand, sparing no feelings, laying herself and her world bare. Crime and corruption fade into a background of misogyny, deceit and human detritus "A thousand cockroaches deep". This is an outstanding, cohesive collection of impeccably crafted poetry from the hand of a poet I return to over and over, whose voice is ever-changing but always challenging, authentic and exciting.

~ Leanne Hanson, author of *Odd Verse Effects* and *Ghost Dreaming*

Track Tales introduces us to a grab bag of characters with crazy superstitions, addicted tragics who lose possessions and families in a fast-paced underworld of cocaine, stand-over merchants and 'easy come – easy go' attitude to life.

~ Rob Walker, author of *Original Clichés* and *Policies & Procedures*

TRACK TALES

poems by
Mercedes
Webb-Pullman

TRUTH SERUM PRESS

First published as a collection October 2017

All poems copyright © Mercedes Webb-Pullman

All rights reserved by the author and publisher. Except for brief excerpts used for review or scholarly purposes, no part of this book may be reproduced in any manner whatsoever without express written consent of the publisher or the author/s.

Truth Serum Press
4 Warburton Street
Magill SA 5072
Australia

Email: truthserumpress@live.com.au
Website: http://truthserumpress.net
Truth Serum Press catalogue: http://truthserumpress.net/catalogue/

Cover design by Matt Potter
Original author photograph by Val Buckland

ISBN: 978-1-925536-35-5

Also available as an eBook
ISBN: 978-1-925536-36-2

Also by Mercedes Webb-Pullman

The Jean Genie (2016)

Collected poems 2008 – 2014 (2015)

Bravo Charlie Foxtrot (2014)

Looking for Kerouac (2014)

Tasseography (2014)

Food 4 Thought (2013)

Ono (2013)

After the Danse (2012)

Numeralla Dreaming (2012)

In memoriam

K. A. Saw

Introduction

I met my second husband in Santa Cruz, 1980. He was on holiday from Sydney, I was living there, studying stained glass construction, working in a bookstore in the Capitola Mall. When I flew back to Australia to spend time with him I was introduced to 'the races'.

Growing up in New Zealand, for me horse races were just an annoying noise on the radio, Saturday afternoons. None of my '70s hippy friends in Sydney went to the races. I'd never been to a racetrack, or had a bet apart from an office pool for the Melbourne Cup.

I was thirty when I got my clerk's licenses: GBOTA, NCA, NSW Trotting Association, Sydney Turf Club and Australian Jockey Club. These meant I could work at Sydney race meetings, whether they were gallops, dogs or trots. (I didn't need a license to work for the SP.)

My husband, Mr. Nasty, mentored me at the tracks. Under his protection, and because we both now worked for a leading bookmaker, I became part of a distinct community with its own culture, language, history, and laws, made up of members of every social and economic strata, a parallel world with a different matrix. Somehow Lady Luck was a Socialist, making all men equal.

It's known as the 'racing fraternity' because it is mostly male. There were few women clerks, among many hundreds, few serious female punters, and only one female dogs bookie. Of course she was known as The Bitch. (The opposite held at the Tote, where the majority of operators were female.)

Already this has changed from the mid '80s, when I stopped working there. I was a penciller then; now, a clerk keys in a bet and a computer issues tickets.

Mr. Nasty has been scratched, as have most of the characters who made up that world. This collection is an attempt to keep their stories alive.

I don't name the bookies I worked for, and no character has their real name. I have taken full advantage of poetic license in descriptions of historical, and hysterical, events.

I've spent the interim 30 years doing many other things. I left Australia in 2008 for New Zealand again, went back to school, graduated from IIML Victoria University Wellington with MA in Creative Writing in 2011.

Now I just write.

Contents

A thousand cockroaches deep / 13

The Green Apple / 15

A fair dinkum champion / 17

From both sides now / 20

The Moose / 23

The Teach / 26

The treachery of numbers / 29

Moving in at Systrum Street / 31

A giant walnut / 35

The Voice of Doom / 38

O Shoshonya! / 41

The day we leave the bag behind / 45

Marrying Mr. Nasty / 49

Ronny the Fish / 53

Buster / 56

The Jet Boat / 60

The stripper on the Rails / 64

The Minister / 67

Family Connections / 70

The man in the Kombi van / 73

Not-So-Fine Cotton / 78

The SP joint / 82

I go to Court, and get busted again / 86

Frank Hardy / 90

The moneybox / 92

The wong Wong / 95

Messing about in boats / 97

Superstitions / 104

Some jockeys are deadly / 106

The ashes / 110

A thousand cockroaches deep

We're working the dogs this night
when The Boss drops by, to dip
some cash from his bags. His kids
come too, three baby millionaires.

He tells me to watch them, keep
them away from dog punters,
the dangerous dark tide that
churns out his cash.

This is sexist bullshit;
I'm a woman,
so I get to mind his kids?

We watch a few races. Dogs don't
do interesting, they just run fast.
That last race may pay for their
higher education, but to the kids
money means nothing.

They live in a world free of cockroaches;
Wentworth Park overflows with them.
They catch sight of one, then more, and
they're bewitched. I show them how to
squash roaches underfoot with
a tap-dance step, while singing.
We make it a competition.

The kids don't want to leave, all complain
as he leads them away. He shoots me
a horrified look from his black
hole-in-the-end-of-a-gun-barrel eyes.

I bet he throws their shoes away
when he gets them home.

The Green Apple

Back before cell phones exist
Aussie Bill Tambole mikes a bookie
we call The Green Apple
at small-town race meetings
each Thursday. Settling takes place
at Claude Fay's in Hornsby, afterwards.

Busy place, it runs hot. Some Smiths,
some on-duty cops, a silk or two,
other assorted criminals, Tommy
'laugh or I'll biff ya' Bristol,
and a gaggle of bookies' clerks.

After a meeting at the Gosford gallops
one day, winner-grinners, we're first
to Claude Fay's, and just for the hell of it,
put an 'Out of Order' sign on the phone
outside the bar.

The Green Apple's strict instructions;
call Aussie Bill with the day's results
at 6 on the dot. Or risk execution.

Green Apple runs in from the traffic jam,
scarlet from exertion and panic
with seconds to spare, reads the sign,
freezes, ashen-faced, trembles
and sinks to his knees. Looks like
he's having a heart attack.

It isn't that funny I guess.

He makes his call on time
but refuses to sit with us
or even talk to us again

and retires that month to run a pub
he buys at Yackandanda,
as far away from racetracks
and the Griffith Mafia
as you can get.

A fair dinkum champion

Working in the radio room one night
sending out price changes on local races
I overhear Glenys and The Prof mention
John the Job so I earwig. He's a mate
I haven't seen lately, but I hear he breeds
a dog, trains it himself, and starts winning.

'Yer' says Glenys. 'He loses his home, his car,
then his missus leaves him. After
his greyhound wins the big race.'

We're astonished. You cop it sweet, losing
when you're on a bad streak, but losing
when you've won? Doesn't make sense.

Glenys settles in, lights up.
She enjoys a good yarn, if it's
someone else's bummer.

'He loves that dog. Spoils it
rotten. He treats it like one of his
grandkids; special diets, massages,
even sleeps on his bed, night before
a race. Takes it to the track in the back
of his car, not in a box. A boof-headed
family pet who runs like the power of piss.

The dog is just too good. Bookies
know it. They won't set a decent price
on it; when it should be six to four,
they offer sixes on. Instead of $660
to win $1000, it costs him $6000.
And still the dog wins. Always a short price.

Then a bookie talks him into a rort.
Run it dead, fix it so the dog can't win
and share the cash that punters place
on the favourite.

They decide which race. Then John
starves his dog, exhausts it, swims it,
runs it on sand a bit more, 'til it's
too tired to win, and no trace of drugs
in its blood. On the night, the bookie
lays it from here to the Black Stump,
at a point over. The money pours in.

They stand to lose a fortune if the dog
gets up, but of course it can't. And
of course it does. He breeds
a fair dinkum champion.

John the Job can't get his head around it.
He owes the bookie all he owns. His dog
frisks around, wanting its pats and treats
for winning. He takes it back to his car
and there on the floor he finds a candy-bar
wrapper. A grandkid must have dropped one
and the dog eats it on the way to the track.'
She pauses, sips bourbon.

The Prof, impatient: 'What does he do? What?'
Glenys smiles. It's like seeing lips on a shark.

'He drives out to Wakehurst Parkway and shoots it.'

From both sides now

I'm penciling 'away' races –
the ones run somewhere else –
at Harold Park this Saturday night.
An Asian woman, middle-aged,
well-dressed, polite, good jewellery,
walks up, smiles, says something
to me I can't understand and shoves
a monkey at me. (That's $500,
a bundle of ten fifties, folded in half
and rubber-banded.)

I never touch cash at the races,
my only job is to keep track of it.
I tell her to ask the bagman for a bet,
he'll take her money, no worries.

Too many spies here – Tax Office,
Treasury, plain clothed police known
as The Consorting Squad, various
pimps, urgers, and other bookies –
for me to be seen taking a wad
of money. Not a good look.
But she's not happy, keeps waving
the monkey at me.

I send a runner to Allen Sung,
ask if he'd mind stepping down
here to help translate. Allen, born
in Sydney of Chinese parents, speaks
with a surprising Ocker accent, but
he speaks fluent Mandarin too, and
gets by in Wu, Min, and Cantonese.

He greets the woman. Her face
lights up. She jabbers away, points
to the bookie's name over our stand,
and on the clerk's money bag, then to
me. Allen fires off a reply, she has
another go, then he sort of bows,
takes the cash, and she walks away.

Allen can't stop grinning. Feels
very strange to see him smile.
A bit frightening.

'She's the aunt of one of your punters,
visiting from Beijing. Your boss helped her
at Randwick today. She borrowed a monkey
from Mary Ann at the payout.'

(Mary Ann, bleached blonde
cougar, wears glasses, has a fat bum
and is twenty years older than me.)

'When she sees you tonight, she checks
the name on the stand, and tries to give back
what you'd lent her.' I tell him I never
saw her before in my life. He nods.

'She confuses you with Mary Ann.
She tells me "They all look the same
to me."'

The Moose

'He's a crawling piece of shit' according
to Mr. Nasty. 'Went to Moocher University.'
The Moose has the sickness, the addiction
that turns life into a chase after the bitch
goddess Lady Luck. She calls him, always,
she's all he hears. He sacrifices to her, does
everything he thinks will win her favour.

Jim, biggest bookie on the tracks, takes
a liking to The Moose and marks his picks
in Moose's racebook for him. If The Moose
follows them, he wins. Same as Jim does.

The first win makes The Moose a genius,
though. He's knows he's lucky. He tosses
Jim's tips out the window, picks his own.
Soon he's broke again.

Once he does it right, sticks to the picks,
wins, and buys himself another house.
'Money's safe in bricks and mortar' he says.
'London to a brick' mutters George. Cynical.
Then The Moose upsets Jim somehow.
The tips stop. The house leaks away,
like a house of water.

I feel sorry for The Moose's wife. We've
never met yet we're linked. I imagine her
at home – a fibro cottage in Marrickville,
dim inside, hushed, everything hidden
behind brown Holland blinds, or covered
in crocheted cream doilies.

Mr. Nasty gives me a sapphire and diamond
ring, with an apology for giving me the clap.
I hate the ring, its rich old-fashioned setting,
the perfect high-set stone. 'Where did you
get it?' Obviously not new.

'The Moose steals it off his bedroom
dresser. His wife's engagement
ring. She thinks she lost it.

I stand him
a monkey on his pick for it, a hot tip
he just has to back.

And it loses.'

The Teach

We work next to each other on the rails
at Randwick. Teach pencils Melbourne,
I'm Brisbane. The boss stands on the bench
above us, in reach of both boards, able
to glance down and read our books.

In the fury of last minute betting he asks
'What are we standing Knackers for?'
Without missing a bet I tell him how much
my book will win or lose if Knackers gets up.

To answer I subtract the payout figure for
that horse from the total held and tell him
'Win five thousand' or 'Lose five thousand'.

I keep a running total in my head of bets laid,
note the rough payout figure on each runner,
write the bet under the right horse, and track
ticket numbers. Teach is faster than me
so he works Melbourne, busier meetings.

He's a high school maths teacher, and knows
odds inside out, but he has the sickness too.
It's killing him. Last week his missus takes
his stake because the kids need new uniforms.
He has to cop it sweet; she's the boss at home.

He's driving down Parramatta Road, heading
for Randwick, radio on to hear scratchings
and early markets. A combination of names
and numbers convinces him he's being shown
the winner of a certain race. At really long odds.

His chance to make a killing and he doesn't
have a stake. But Luck has stopped him at lights
right beside a 'Cash Paid' car dealer. It's a sign.

He sells his car and catches a train to the races
with a pocket full of cash, convinced he's a
genius. This is how the sickness works.

Some are immune, most catch it. Luck
has nothing to do with smarts. As many
Supreme Court judges, bankers, priests,
politicians, lawyers, coppers, businessmen,
and academics, as bare-footed day-laborers,
they jostle and shove in their blood frenzy
to claim the bitch in the final seconds of betting.

I see it in his eyes, wild, irrational,
but totally alive, willing the minutes away
until his race jumps, caught up in the glory
of a sure thing, home at a long price. Except
of course it runs ninth.

By the next meeting he's living in a single room
in the Cross, eating at Food Courts. His shirt is
clean, but not ironed. Still, he's full of life, news
of a roughie that's going to get up today. 'Just
look at its name; all the vowels are in the right
order, and there are three letters the same.'

The treachery of numbers

When I work my first race
The Boss asks me for the result.
I say 'won fifty thousand', and
grin. He gimlets me with his eyes,
black and dangerous like the hole
in the end of a gun barrel.

He must have lost on the race
but my cash bets book wins.
The loss must be in the nod book,
clients who bet on credit with a nod
and settle with cash at City Tats later.

When I look, the nod book
shows a win too. Something
doesn't feel right.

I notice when some people bet
on the nod, our prices drop
as if thousands had been laid
but the bet is in hundreds.

The Judge asks for $20 on Vagabond.
Gold-toed boots flashing, Mr. Nasty is off
to back it back at half a point over odds.
Donny the Fish rushes to take Vagabond
with the field quinella, field and field
trifecta, on the Tote. The Judge is
down for $20 only.

The Boss must calculate mentally,
automatically, instantly, so much cash,
so many credit bets; multiply some
by ten. Some by a thousand. Somehow
he keeps a running total, changing odds
to cover how much each horse will cost him
if it wins, no matter what the books say.

No wonder he glares at me.
I don't grin at work at the races again.
You can't really tell
when you're winning.

Moving in at Systrum Street

Here we are, carting clothes and bedding
from the car to the just-purchased house,
inner Sydney, two-floor bald-faced terrace
one room wide, two deep, so small if we park
outside the Fairlane overlaps. Empty street,
2 a.m. traffic hum from Broadway. We're tired,
just worked three meetings in a day and night.

No lights working upstairs; we carry candles,
clothes, dump stuff everywhere, stumble back
'til it's all inside. Organize a bed.

Loud knock on the front door. Mr. Nasty opens.
Dark blue uniforms, two police; a fat sergeant,
a woman with a face you could crack granite on,
both middle-aged. Sergeant's the one barking.

Mr. Nasty explains we've just bought the place, we're moving in after work. Cop says 'Prove it.' You don't get a certificate on settlement. Your lawyer sends stuff later. Bank has the title deed.

'Who owns the car?' It's registered in my name. 'Where's your driver's license?' I grab my bag from the floor, open it so the cop can't see in; for sure he'd ask about the bricks of $20 notes. We don't want to be talking about them at all. Mr. Nasty passes my license, introduces himself.

The cops, outside on the footpath, have clear sightline through to the back door. Someone knocks. I'm shocked. The back gate is locked, we checked before bringing stuff in. It's surrounded by brick walls two meters high. The cop tells me to open it.

Into the room bounds death, a kid with
a gun, pointed at me. He screams, shaking
so badly he can barely stand, jaw clenched.
I see muscles knot as time slows. We both
freeze in place. He's a policeman.

I watch the barrel, the black hole that just
swallowed time. If I sneeze he'll kill me.
The sergeant talks, calms him without
approaching. His white knuckles, finger
still on the trigger. We're on pause, waiting
until 'Put it down, son. Put it down' slowly
the kid lowers his gun. We feel death leave.

I can move again. We learn why they came:
neighbours, fearing squatters, reported lights
in an empty house. They sent a team of three;
one to run around the back, scale the fence
and grab anyone coming out the back door
while two knock at the front.

The kid takes so long to climb the fence
he panics, adrenalin-pumped, thinks he's
missing something. When I open the door
he leaps, gun drawn, into a situation not
what he expects. His mind can't process it.

Some have trouble chewing and walking
at the same time. They teach this one how
to draw his gun, but not when, and never
show him he can put it away.

'No point in being pissed off.' Mr. Nasty
after they leave. 'If you lay a complaint
they'll make your life hell. They're from
Regent Street, the station where police
fuck-ups from all over the city get sent.
Everyone calls it Reject Street. You're
alive, aren't you? Just cop it sweet.'

A giant walnut

At six o'clock Mr. Nasty remembers he's
invited dinner guests; I take saucepans
to No Names, back in fifteen with food:
home-made bolognaise, fettuccine,
salad greens, focaccia.

I leave dinner on the back seat
to open the front door;
it needs two hands. Raised voices
from the living room. Mr. Nasty doing his

"Mate... mate ..."

to four angry men, Greek gamblers
we meet Thursdays, after race meetings,
at Claude Fay's in Hornsby.
They want repayment
of a substantial loan.

Italian food. Insulting? I set out
olives, walnuts, and cheese, find
the Giannatsi ouzo a punter brought
back from Plomari, fill glasses, and listen.

Mr. Nasty is back in Sydney a week
after a month's ski holiday in Austria
or so he tells me.

Surprise!

He borrows $40,000 from these men,
flies to Switzerland, from there to Peru,
buys a kilo of cocaine and loses it in a
very complicated story.

That's what the phone calls from
Avis in Lima Peru were all about.

He now owes the Greeks $50,000,
increasing by $10,000 weekly. They
offer to break my legs, leave him
able to earn, working hot at the races.

I go to bed, forgetting food.
Things get busy. I need three jobs.
We have to sell the Fairlane.
I find the saucepans still there
on the back seat, hidden under
newspapers and betting sheets.
Colonies of mould and fungus
cover the bolognaise
with putrid blue/green threads
in the shape of a brain.
Or maybe it's a giant
walnut.

The Voice of Doom

Weekdays he works in the State Premier's
Department. Has a lot of tug with unions,
handy for the Boss who has construction
companies. Weekends he clerks at the races.

He suffers from the sickness. Maybe that's
why he's still single. Charming, confident,
snazzy dresser; always in a good bag of fruit,
with worn running shoes though, not the
Gucci loafers you expect.

Saturdays he's a runner, sent at speed
with a wad of cash to back back a runner
with other bookies, if The Boss is holding
too much for it. Before the price goes off.
One intense minute max each race. The rest
of the meeting, like me, he watches and listens.

He hates the frenzy he forces his way through,
punters at fever pitch, the shove and jostle,
sweat and bad breath, the dips working hot,
the noise. He hates being told what to do, too,
but he's shackled by his need for a win,
to control Lady Luck. That buzz means more
than money. Punters or bookies, they're all
adrenalin junkies, with the promise of a fix
every twenty minutes.

One Saturday at Randwick I lean on a wall
in a patch of sun, between races, and I spot
The Voice of Doom walk behind a Moreton Bay
fig tree near the main exit, out of sight of
the stand. He stays there for the broadcast.
Then he wanders off.

At dinner I ask Mr. Nasty 'What's the strength
on The Voice of Doom hiding behind the fig tree?'

'He's a silly cunt, that one. He'll do it on the wrong race one day, get himself shot. Instead of putting money on the runner The Boss tells him to back, he fields it himself. He walks behind the tree, puts The Boss's cash in his pocket. He's careful about which race he does it on. Must be a busy meeting, too, lots of cash flying around. Back at the stand he throws picked-up tickets into the bag, he's taking the odds to no one looking at them 'til after the meeting. No way to tell what happened by then, the bag's full of tickets at the end of the day, with no way to know who went wrong.'

'And the tree? Why listen to the race there?'

'If the runner does get up he's still got two choices. He can go back to the stand, throw the money back into the bag and say 'Couldn't get on' or he can be out of there, into his car, to the airport and gone. Toss of a coin. The only time he ever feels alive."

O Shoshonya!

Saturdays, between the gallops and the dogs,
The Boss clerks often eat together, usually at
The Old Tai Pen in Chinatown, Bogarts on
Glebe Point Road, or Tilly Devines, where
Colin the owner cooks the best filet mignon.
We go there after work too, chill out. By then

Colin is pissed, one of his three daughters
or his wife is running the bar, loud music and
mayhem play, a wine bar that sells everything.
His wife comes across like a North Shore matron
but she's as outrageous as he is. She helps run
the last bar, complete with boobs and lap dancing.
It pays for their girls' good schools, music lessons.
He lost the liquor licence, unspecfied breach of
regulations. Now he operates a wine bar licence
selling any booze for as long as he gets away with it.

One of Mr. Nasty's mates, Paul the Kiwi chippy,
dates Kate the oldest daughter. We're guests in
their Hunters Hill home, we play with their Afghan
hound Sheik.

Colin gets pissed and holds impromptu talent quests
at Tillys. He starts, singing 'Plastic Jesus', always forgets
the words after 'riding on the dashboard of my car',
hopeless Irish drunk, impossible not to laugh. Someone
from the crowd takes his guitar, does a number, we heckle
or applaud until Colin gets back in there, starts crooning
'O Shoshonya! O Shoshonya!' again and again, until
he starts crying. He calls it the most beautiful love song
he's ever heard, it's Russian. All he remembers of it
is 'O Shoshonya!'

Mr. Nasty, Paul and I take them to the Snowy Mountains,
the girls to ski, parents to tour Eucumbene trout farm.

We're through the gear hire first, fast, early morning
at Guthega. Nasty, Paul and the two oldest girls head
for the lift, to meet back here in two hours. I take
my charge, put her into a two-hour beginners class
and take a few runs down the rope tow. Cold crisp snow,
dry and delicious to my edges, nice little set of moguls
I keep running 'til the snow softens, and it's time to
meet the others.

My charge, the only one missing. We search, ask,
finally track her down to the medical centre
where she's prone, knee fat and bandaged,
in pain and apologetic for making a fuss.
She's standing there on skis, waiting to be
shown what to do, moves and her skis start
to run. She doesn't know how to stop.
People shout at her, she gets faster
and faster, and falls over a bank
into a gully, wrenching her knee,
skis still on, upside down.
She had to be rescued by Ski Patrol,
in a banana boat.

That happens five minutes after I leave her. She's having
abandonment issues, three hours later, but she knows
we'll find her.

Colin and the Mrs. bring a box from the trout farm, meals
for the kitchen at Tillys I think as we drop them home later,
the girls almost asleep, Colin and the Mrs. pissed.
We're going back for lunch next day.

We're met by Sheik the Afghan, on the grass, front legs
splayed as he leans into the pool, scoops mouthfuls
from a layer of what turns out to be young trout.
'I told him it wouldn't work' says the Mrs.

'He wanted to grow them up in the pool, that's what
they live in at the trout farm, so he bought that box
of 500 fingerlings, and dropped them in here last night.
He's sure they were alive then, says he saw them moving.
He threw chopped liver in there too, to feed them.

He's not sure what killed them though, the trip,
the liver, or the chlorine in the water.'

From inside, through an open window, floats a mournful
'O Shoshonya!'

'At least Sheik likes the fish.' The Mrs. ignores him.
'Probably the most expensive meal he's ever had.

And that's counting those freshwater lobsters.'

The day we leave the bag behind

Each race day the leather bookie's bag
sits ready by the tower's back door, beside
the replenished aluminium ticket case,
last things to pick up on the way to work.

This Saturday we leave early, with time
to drop my visiting sister at the station
on the way to Royal Randwick. We drive
from Palm Beach to the city along the coast,
give her a last view of surf beaches and sun,
which takes longer than planned; traffic jams
near Manly and Dee Why, but we make it to
the bookie's car park right on time, an hour
before the first.

Time to set up the stand, check scratchings
on the printed runners lists, already thinking
ahead as Mr. Nasty reaches into the back for
bag and case, realizes he's left them behind.

Takes an hour to drive Randwick to Palm Beach
in traffic like this, noon on a summer Saturday,
but Mr. Nasty is determined to get there and back
in that time. We work our way at speed through
Anzac Parade. I kneel on the front seat, watching
through the rear window for cops. No seat belt
reaches this position; if Mr. Nasty brakes suddenly
I'll be in the shit but I must do it. It's my fault,
my sister who upset his routine.

He weaves around slower cars, cursing at traffic,
a continual tirade, I wish I was recording this,
things about goats and grandmothers I've never
heard before. He's driving like a champion.

The city looks strange, vanishing behind me
instead of opening up ahead. Constantly, fading
horns, tyre screeches, I'm glad I can't see what's
happening, only what has already, clutching hard
to the seat back, relaxing on Wakehurst Parkway,
Mr. Nasty cajoling the car 'Go, you heap of shit.'

We must be doing near a hundred miles an hour,
not slowing to swing north and back into traffic,
weaving, ducking, we're through Avalon village
onto Whale Beach Road, up our shared driveway
with prayers no neighbours are coming down,
so fast the car bottoms out but we're home.

Mr. Nasty exits, Peter the houseboy holds out bag
and tickets from the back door, back in the car
and off, time elapsed 28 minutes.

We might just make it, no time to think though,
just Go! Go! the road twisting away behind us. I
feel sick, sway around, car horns, curses, red lights
run, still no cops, I'm panting from holding my breath,
keep forgetting to breathe, totally focused until
we pull into the bookie's carpark again, just behind
The Boss, who frowns and wonders why we're late,
Lucky you made it in time. He doesn't know how close
he was to not fielding the first because his number one man
forgot to bring tickets and bag. Mr. Nasty sprints
to the stand, early markets not yet up. My race
doesn't jump for another hour,
I go to the nearest bar and down a neat scotch,
then another. Tremors slowly leave my hands, heart beat
slows to normal.

I've never felt so frightened in my life, yet so removed from it at the same time. The sun, the breeze, the people, everything I see now so pin-point precious to me, I'm alive, and horny as hell suddenly. Man, that was exhilirating.

Marrying Mr. Nasty

I wake slowly, our first married morning. Sun
through our bedroom window, parrots clatter
in the garden. At first I forget the night before.
Then I remember, groan loud enough to wake
Mr. Nasty. His eyes open but he doesn't move.
Neither do I. We lie side by side, fully clothed,
on top of the quilt, like discarded toys. I'm still
wearing wedding dress and high heels.

My head pains at the sound of my groan; now
the rest of my body complains.

A combination of too much champagne, I think,
maybe someone dropped acid in the fruit punch,
a lot of good Nepalese temple balls did the rounds,
and copious fine white lines, and rage, which will
always take a high that bit over the top. I'm so angry
I'm petrified.

The wedding part of it goes OK. A celebrant stands
on the back deck steps, guests sit or lean or lounge
as she recites the Desiderata and words that marry us.
Dark by now, paper lanterns shine from our trees
as everyone cheers at the end, a wave of good feeling;
I'm grinning like a child. Friends surround Mr. Nasty.

I chat to his mother and her sisters, weirdly the same
face, short ladies, pink apple cheeks, black button eyes,
guardians of the wedding presents display upstairs
according to some unspoken protocol. I know nothing
of the intricacies of weddings, this is only my second.
My first husband organizes the first; I just turn up.

So the sisters – they don't come up to my shoulders –
lead me to the tower steps, the presents. A bathroom
door hangs half open. Or half closed. I push it; there's
Mr. Nasty, shoulders to the wall. Janice, my brother's wife,
my sister-in-law, kneels with his cock in her mouth.
We've been married exactly fifteen minutes. So that's
how long my marriage lasts, really. Everything after that
is just botched exits.

Of course his mother and aunties see it too. They fluff
and cluck like hens at the sight of a hawk. I'm not angry
he's having sex with someone else. It's more to do with
time, and place.

I get drunk on Roderer Cristal then switch to the punch
Peter the houseboy mixes from white spirits, champagne,
tropical fruit. He and his squeeze, in tuxes, serve guests
food and booze. They're having a ball. Everyone is.
Our friends don't know each other yet. Peter sticks
labels on as they arrive, with their names,
no introductions needed. I wear one saying 'Bride'.

Sue helps me drink. She's my bridesmaid twice.
(My brother gives me away both times. He takes
Janice home.) Ski mates mingle well with the
racing crowd. Sue tells The Boss's sister about
a weekend when she doesn't go to Woodstock.

I meet Sue working in Thredbo. We keep in touch, the Hole
in the Head gang from Thredbo summers of the '70s. She
thinks I take it all too seriously. She thinks it's hilarious, with
Macbeth's witches as witnesses. But she's a psych nurse.

The final ritual, cutting the cake. A croquembouche pair;
lots of guests and we want everyone to have some.
Mr. Nasty's brother, a chef, caters as his gift. Of course
the food is superb. I remember some chicken. Mr. Nasty
looks a bit edgy, standing next to me, like he's not sure
what I'm going to do next.

We each grasp a bun from a pyramid top, break it free
from the spiky caramel glaze, and eat it in one bite.
The filling is liqueur custard – Cointreau? Grand
Marnier? – croquembouche therapy. The guests
help themselves. The cakes vanish in minutes.

The party breaks down. I wander off to bed.
Honeymoon starts tomorrow – how can I go
to the States for six weeks with this prick? How do I
go about getting out of this? That's when I fall asleep.

That's what I wake up with, anyway. A stale thought,
left over from the night before. My wedding night.

Ronny the Fish

He wears a bag for The Boss, short man but he towers over the punters on his fold-up-and-carry clerk's stool. He's up a level, they'd overwhelm him otherwise. He grabs their cash, checks it, drops it in the bag as he calls the bet for the penciller, scribbles the ticket, hands it to the punter, takes the next notes held up, biggest bets first, repeat. He's patient, fast, accurate. I like working with him, good pace.

Quiet man, my father's age, bald on top, sides clipped close, grey stubble. Wears rimless specs with gold arms, works at the city fish markets, where he smokes fish and roe for Greek restaurants. He brings us gifts, purses of treasure, masses of red-gold eggs glistening. I squish them on buttered toast for breakfast, a spritz of lemon juice; better than caviar, fresher. We're friends for ages before one of the Watsons tells me Fish was a prisoner of Japan, WWII, captured in Singapore, sent to Changi, from there to a camp in Burma. He never mentions it so I ask him.

They build a railway by hand, through the jungle. He says
his mates drop around him like flies. He wants to die too,
join them. He volunteers for the typhoid tent, holds men
so they don't die alone, tries to catch what kills them but
he can't.

He talks about the mate with ulcers eating his legs. No
medication or sanitation, no way to stop the process,
pain. He can't walk, the ulcers go down to his bones, so
Donny the Fish carries him down to the creek, seats him
so his legs hang in the water. Tiny fish in there can eat
away the decaying flesh. Then he carries him uphill
back to his stretcher.

Some things, shaving each day with half a cup of water
or the way he eats rice, show how close his war still is.

'What keeps you alive? What do you do that others don't?'
He's got every right to tell me to mind my own business.
We're doing an 'away' race, dogs at West Kick-a-tin-along,
it's raining, no punters interested, a quiet night for us.
He stares straight ahead as if the scene before him is not
the one I see. He looks like a blind monk, or a prophet.

'Every night before I go to sleep I remember the last
Christmas dinner we have together; everyone comes
to our place, aunts, uncles, cousins, grandmothers,
with my Mum and Dad, my sister, two brothers and me.
I remember where we all sit around the table, what we're
all wearing, my mother's apron, my grandmother's foxes
hanging on the peg by the door. I remember what we eat.
Sometimes I can even hear what we say to each other.
I go back in time, away from what's around me.

Each night before I go to sleep I go home for Christmas.
Their faces light up to see me, my mother gives me a kiss,
I shake hands with Dad, cousin Julie starts coughing,
Aunt Janet slaps her on the back, 'Something gone down
the wrong way has it?' and dinner goes on exactly as I
remember it. I think that's what saves me. My mother's
best apron, and her kiss.'

Buster

He's another rough diamond who always
treats me well, a go-for who fills in for clerks
if needed. He wears a bag, though he's slow
writing tickets, and won't pencil, though he
probably can. He just doesn't like it. He'd
rather be a runner, backing back along
the rows of bookies, standing in line
at the Tote windows, bringing news,
gossip, tea and sandwiches back to the Boss,
acting as his eyes and ears. The Boss never
leaves the stand, at a meeting.

He also lugs bags and tickets to the tracks,
and takes them away again. He's a hero
but never mentions war. Merchant Marine,
six times his ships are sunk; a real survivor.
The Boss treats him like a good luck charm.
He's always around in the background,
a security blanket. He knows more about
the family than anyone else who's
not part of it, a two-way implicit trust.

He brings extra cash to the pay-out clerk,
takes charge of his bag at meeting's end
when it's almost empty of cash, full of tickets
whose torn-off corners show they've been paid.
I can imagine headaches involved in balancing
cash, reconciling it with book and credit bets,
keeping a check on the honesty of clerks by
the difference between what amount should
be there, and what actually is.

Between races one day, a slow one, we chat.
He tells me none of the systems we use are
fool-proof. I'm intrigued. 'No' he says
'No matter how hard they try, there's always
human error. Why, one Sunday ...' and he's
reminiscing, unusual for him so I listen.

'I always start a fire in the Boss's backyard
incinerator on a Sunday, to burn paid tickets
once they've calculated how the day went.
Makes sure they can't be used to pay out
twice. Big day at Randwick on Saturday,
big night at Wentworth Park. Serial numbers
of the tickets jump all over the place, so I'm
waiting for a while. I keep the fire alight with
sheets of old fields until the Boss brings bags.

'Here, burn these, Buster, and we'll go to the
Manadarin Club for lunch.' This means
he's had a good day and when the Boss
is happy, everyone is.

So I upend the first bag into the incinerator,
give the tickets a stir with my stick, to keep
them burning, pick up the next bag to empty,
when something makes me look into it. Maybe
it's the weight. It feels too heavy. The bag
is full of money, packed into bricks the way
they do it, all twenties; each brick is two
thousand dollars, and there are dozens. I'm
about to burn them. Boss hardly thanks me,
though he's won around thirty grand more
than he thought. So you see, love,
even the best can make mistakes.'

'You never think of pocketing it yourself?
After all, it wouldn't be missed.' Buster is
aghast. 'The thought never crosses my mind'
he says. 'There are things in the world more
valuable than cash. Like being able to look
the Boss in the eye. And yourself, in the
mirror in the morning, shaving.'

The Jet Boat

Long before I'm around Mr. Nasty scores a jet boat
and blows up the motor, 351 Cleveland V8, 800 horse,
on the Hawkesbury by driving over oyster bed frames
on the way home from the Gosford gallops one dusk.
The bed isn't there when he goes up the river.
He doesn't think about tides.

'Flames out both sides of the block! You wouldn't
believe the bang!' Lucky the jets aren't damaged.

Old Silver's brother's mate fixes it in his workshop
in Cronulla. He wants to buy it. Made of aircraft
aluminium, purpose-built lobster boat from W.A.,
the hot rod of working boats in the State. Nothing
in the hull but a seat near the steering wheel, and
an engine covering; it can carry a shitload of lobsters.
It falls into Mr. Nasty's kick at the races one day.

He uses it for work sometimes; Gosford is 15 minutes
from Palm Beach by water, two hours by road.
'This can outrun the Water Police' Mr. Nasty boasts,
but so far he hasn't had to test it.

Before we use it to go to the Gosford gallops, he
puts it in Pittwater at Palm Beach Marina, shows me
what the boat can do. I'm on board when he tries to
make it leap out of the water and spin a 360 in the air.

He says he's done it before, tells me to hold on and
brace. I clutch the edge of the side. He spins the wheel,
boat lurches, the steering wheel spokes shatter.
Mr. Nasty hurtles into the exposed wheel hub
and breaks a few ribs. We only just don't overturn.

There's enough spoke stub to steer the boat, which
I have to do. He has broken ribs. We limp to the marina.
I'm secretly glad to postpone the trip to Gosford.
But the day does arrive.

The journey is uneventful, a jittery rattle because water
is so solid at that speed, constantly smacking the hull.
Wind blows my hair back, salty taste, hypnotic engine
like a Harley roaring down a narrow brick alley in the city.
Slowly, from the haze we're headed towards,
land looms and solidifies.

We've been told we can moor for the day
at the wharf built into the side of the Yacht Club.
Dining room and bar upstairs. Mr. Nasty must
manouevre at speed, or it's impossible to steer
using jets so he sort of slaloms in towards the wharf
with a flourish, ready to turn and come alongside.
But the jets cut out suddenly and the prow hits
the pilings quite hard.

The building sways. Above us a window slides open.
'What the fuck d'ya think you're doing?' the manager
I guess. The one we're supposed to slip a twenty,
to keep an eye on the jet boat while we're at work.
'Sorry, mate, sorry, didn't mean to do that, the jets
just cut out on me.' It makes no difference.

'Fuck off, you're not tying up here. You're not members.
Crazy fucker.' The head vanishes.

We wallow around in the water a bit. Mr. Nasty yells
to Old Silver, who's come to take us from here to the track.
Silver takes off his runners and socks, rolls pants legs up
and wades in, above his knees when he reaches the boat.

Mr. Nasty keeps thrusting the drive lever back and forth;
engine roars, but no water through the jets. Mr. Nasty
swears a new stanza about the goat and the grandmother
while Silver gropes around under the boat for the jet intakes.
Mr. Nasty is spitting chips. We can't be late for the first,
he can't leave the boat here but he can't go anywhere else.

The veins that signal migraine start throbbing
on his forehead, he's very tense when Old Silver
shouts 'Got it!', fumbles under the boat, hauls out
a plastic fertilizer sack. The jet intakes suck it up
and there it sticks, seals them. Now the rooster-tails
reappear.

'Meet you at the marina' to Silver. We're off flat chat again,
moor at the marina without problems, Silver picks us up,
drives really fast, we'll just be in time to field the first.
Mr. Nasty still fumes 'That'd be right, stalled by a shit bag,
piece of shit' 'At least you don't wreck
the Cleveland again' I offer. He glares.

Whump whump whump as a helicopter passes over and
lands in the outfield. Jockeys from the city pile out.
Mr. Nasty stares at the chopper, far too thoughtfully.
'I wonder how much …' he says. I stop listening.

The stripper on the Rails

Mr. Nasty's birthday looms. He hardly needs things; portable valuables like jewellery, watches, cameras, all pass through his hands at the races as punters, down on their luck, stake valuables like their grandfather's solid gold repeater watch and chain, family heirloom, on a sure thing, and lose. Restaurants, booze, everyday recreational pursuits; nothing special in them for a gift.

He likes cheeky, he likes to laugh, so I send a birthday Stripper-Gram to where we work on the Rails at Royal Randwick, an hour before the first race. She'll be gone before The Boss arrives. Christmas is only weeks away; Danni arrives in a sort of Santa suit, if Santa wore red satin, plus feather boa. Long blonde hair, green eyes, she sets her portable music on the bench, switches on.

Shirley Bassey booms out 'Big Spender', Danni grins,
bumps and grinds, smooth dancer, flirting with the
boa as she loses her jacket, reveals perfect tits in a
red top, bare shoulders outlined in fluffy white fur.
She peels each glove off, finger by finger, as a crowd
of punters jostle and drool.

Danni's really grinding it out now, toned body, totally
in time with the music, a little shrug and tug, the top's
gone, leaving a tiny Chrismas bra only just holding her
as she shimmies out of her skirt, looking back over her
shoulder, winking, but no one sees.

They're all focused on a most perfect pair of buttocks,
divided only by a thong, and a groan passes around
as she strokes the boa back and forth between her legs,
muscles rippling with the dance. Danni flexes, rolls;
electric tension as she turns again.

Without losing pace, just as Shirley hits the final line 'Spend a little time with me', she shimmies out of the bra, and red white and green tassels on her nipples start to move; now she twirls the Christmas tassels as the punters cheer and roar and laugh, incredulous that this beautiful almost naked woman is there among them, and she pulls on her coat, grabs her music, and Danni's gone.

Mr. Nasty loves it. He's in such a good mood he wins on the day. When a shot of him watching Danni do her act appears in the Herald, he doesn't mind. At all.

The Minister

Mr. Nasty's born into a racing family, his grandfather a jockey killed in a fall. 'Only mark on him was a hoof print in the middle of his forehead.' His Dad's a bookie, works mainly on dogs, specializes in all-up doubles, until Lady Luck shits on him too. He can't put enough heat on the nod punters who won't pay their losing bets.

Being a bookie means knowing how to ride the wave. Money. Sometimes you get dumped. Mr. Nasty tells me he sees his mother chase the workman, to stop him from turning off their gas before she cooks tea for her sons. She cries a lot. That night his father comes home from the dogs driving a brand new American car, huge, with white-wall tyres. Mr. Nasty thinks this kind of up/down is how everyone lives. He's born on a Saturday, race day, so his father doesn't see his first-born son until Sunday.

One of his Dad's nod punters works his way up; union rep into local government, a seat in the State elections, moves from back bencher to a Ministry because he's well-connected. 'More front than Myers' says Mr. Nasty. The Minister is another victim of the disease.

'Dad could wall-paper the shit-house with The Minister's settling cheques. Prick always expects to collect cash, though, if he backs a winner.'

We're coming home from Wentworth Park one night, stopped at a red light, waiting to turn right into Harris Street, hardly any traffic, and a car flashes past us on the inside lane, totally ignores the red traffic light, and slams into a car half-way over the intersection, catching its rear end, sending it spinning down three luckily empty lanes. Mr. Nasty sprints over to see if he can help.

Blood's pouring over the face of the first driver, from a cut on his forehead, it's The Minister, and he's totally pissed. The other driver's half-conscious and hurt, he's freaking. An ambulance arrives, then cops. They take Mr. Nasty's details as a witness. Early next day a suit arrives. He wants to take a statement. He's The Minister's solicitor. I leave them to it.

In the wash, it seems that The Minister has a green light,
the car he hits runs a red, and the high alcohol content
in The Minister's blood comes from swigging on a bottle of
Scotch, in shock, handed to him by a bystander while he's
waiting for the cops to arrive. Two witnesses back this up:
Mr. Nasty, and a punter from the dogs who happens to be
walking home along Harris Street at the time.
The other driver cops it sweet, has no memory
of the event, gets a ticket for running a red light,
plus a new car and a small bank account.

'What if he kills that kid instead of breaking his head?'
I ask Mr. Nasty.

'You just don't understand the way things work
at the races.' He's right. I don't. I'm learning, though.

Months later a punter asks Mr. Nasty for a favour, can he
set up a meeting with The Minister, on the QT?
The punter's son jumps through the wrong window,
ends up in a brickstone university up country. By now
The Minister is Minister of Prisons, and he's glad to help.

In fact he's glad to help a few prisoners, as long as someone
comes up with a few thousand good reasons why. Mr. Nasty
cops a ten per cent finder's fee from The Minister, and
for a while everyone is sweet.

Family Connections

His name's well-known, but it's his uncle The Snake or his younger rabid cousins that people hear about. He's private. Same age as Mr. Nasty, a bookie father too, they both know their way around a track before they leave school. Opposite ends of the scale, ant and leviathan, clerk and bookmaker. Maths is the same. They understand each other.

Once upon a time there are three brothers who stay at home, out of service, during the Second World War. Somehow they make a lot of money. Opinion divides about where it comes from; government supply contracts, or financing a shipload of whisky to Sydney, escorted by the navy, when imports can't get through. Even empty bottles are worth money, for refilling with a bathtub white moonshine, tinted with cold tea.

One thing for sure, the brothers end up with a shitload of money. All they have at the start is their father's Eastern Suburbs pub. The smart brother forms a trust, makes them all beneficiaries, invests in real estate, buys them a house each, expensive suburbs, buys more land, more pubs, more houses, blocks of flats, they're all supported and the cash flows in.
Then the smart brother dies.

The survivors pounce on the trust. Crows on roadkill. Court case follows court case for years, alliances alter, set some against others for life. The dead man's sons resent control by uncles. The Snake (they say he eats human flesh, once at Med School) battles his brother for overall control. One nephew, sent by his uncles to boarding school unwillingly, to get him out of the way, sends a letter bomb to the headmaster. A young priest has his hands blown off. A hush fund goes into action.

This generation spreads the family franchise, from owning, training and racing thoroughbreds through imports of Charolais to the supply of blue metal for road construction in suburban subdivisions where the trust owns and develops land in partnership with the government. This generation moves out of pubs.

Rich kids, born privileged. None of them trusts the rest
of the family. Witnesses to signatures may or
may not have deprived the trust of certain assets,
to the detriment of certain of the beneficiaries,
and the benefit of others. The next generation
don't really care. They're petrol-heads, ride bikes
instead of horses, chuck wheelies, ripping up their
unused tennis courts where they learn to drive.

Another block of North Shore units surfaces;
hidden by the dead brother, bought with money
from the Family Trust. Smart brother rips off
the other two right from the start. In their turn
they rip off his sons, their nephews. So it goes,
a dinkum dynasty through three generations.
'Shirt sleeves to shirt sleeves' mutters George darkly.

I see an image of a snake, swallowing the tail
of another snake. It swallows the tail of a third,
that swallows the first snake's tail. All three
spin together, conjoined, devouring each other,
feeding each other, carried along towards death
on the backs of horses; first, whisky, the White Horse,
then the Sport of Kings, the race horse.

The man in the Kombi van

After a long day at Wyong we're heading home,
down the Pacific Highway. The Boss has a good day.
Mr. Nasty wears a black cloud which means he's lost
or something's gone wrong. I don't ask. We're near
Crows Nest. A rackety Kombi van cuts into our lane
without signalling. Mr. Nasty has to take evasive action,
enough to focus his mood. 'Look at that silly prick.
If I couldn't drive I'd have hit him and it'd be my fault
because I'm behind him. Maybe he does it on purpose.'

Mr. Nasty sometimes has paranoid fantasies about being
followed. His father has been held up at gunpoint by one
of the Smiths, after a day when his bag wasn't even full.
'Maybe he thinks I'm carrying cash for The Boss which
he does between the day gallops and the night
dogs or trots. We sit down to eat each Saturday night with
$50,000 in the bag. 'Maybe he wants to rob me.'

I'm uneasily aware of the shotgun that sits, broken, over the drive shaft hump on the car floor between our seats. Lucky we don't have any shells for it. He pulls level with the Kombi, blares his horn, chucks the fingers at its driver, tells him how many degrees lower than a goat he is. And all his female antecedents too. Pointless to try to do anything, he'll run out of puff soon enough.

We're sitting right on the Kombi's tail now. Mr. Nasty jams the horn down and holds it, the Kombi suddenly turns left without signalling and Mr. Nasty follows it off the highway, round a corner, watches it pull into the open car space under a unit block. 'He's chicken, he's trying to do a runner on me now' and he parks, grabs the shotgun, leaps from the car, fizzing with anger. He's not usually a fool. He knows you don't brandish an empty gun at a stranger. This may be the last stupid thing he ever does.

He's parked near a streetlight. His shadow grows
across the road as he walks. It's a scene from a Western,
The Showdown, or from a noir detective movie.
Mr. Nasty's constant tirade, at first full vent, slows,
eases, even his body language changes, he's happy
when he gets back in the car, relaxed. 'See what that
silly prick does? He pisses himself!' he laughs,
turns left, back on the highway headed home.

Couple of months later we're on the deck in the sun
when cops arrive with the Armed Offenders Squad.
He's under arrest for firearm offenses, taken away
to Manly Police Station. I follow, ready to post bail.
Sergeant wants to take a statement from me. 'You know
he's admitted everything that happened when he
pointed a gun at this citizen.' So I tell the story,
Mr. Nasty gets released on bail, and we go home.
'Dumb fucking pigs. Thicker than two planks.'

He's grinning. Seems the Kombi driver, unfortunate to be
in the same space, unaware of malfunctioning indicators,
reports assault by a gunman. He gives
Mr. Nasty's description and car rego.
Some young cop, keen as mustard,
follows up, traces the rego to a car fleet
lease manager for a company which
leads him to The Boss and ultimately
Mr. Nasty, who, this genius cop decides,
based solely on the fact that he works
at the races, and he has a gun, is
The Boss's Enforcer.
Armed Offenders Squad photograph us for six weeks;
at the races, at home on the deck, on the yacht,
even shopping at the Palm Beach grocery store.

'They got heaps of photos of my tattoos, even' marvels
Mr. Nasty, but that's not surprising to me, they're on each
cheek of his arse, two W's so when he chucks a brown-eye
they spell WoW, and he's always taking his pants off.

Mr. Nasty goes to court on the day without a solicitor.
'Don't need one' he says. The case is called, police confer,
withdraw the charges, case dismissed. That's it.
'How do you know their only witness is a no-show?'
I'm curious. He laughs. 'Always someone who listens
to good reasons. It only took a thousand good reasons
for a clerk to make an honest mistake, send the citizen
a wrong court date. Not much he can do about that.'

The Boss is not at all impressed by the whole fiasco.

Not-So-Fine Cotton

I'm pencilling at Randwick, the Rails, working
on Brisbane races, Eagle Farm meeting that day.
There's a sort of low buzz going around the track,
'Someone's got a fix in' but that's not unusual,
there's always some cheating going on, I'm not
curious about who or what or where, just keep
my head down and listen.

Punters want to back some knackery-bait in a race
at Eagle Farm. The early market shows fifty to one,
but The Boss doesn't want a cent of it. Even I know
something's off when every punter and his brother
wants to back the same long-priced roughie. It's got
no form, no wins, no chance of winning. Some owner
with more money than sense keeps sending it around
the tracks, and as long as it's registered, all fees paid,
it can run. Even though trainers hate wasting time,
it's owners with dreams who pay their bills.

Opening market has Fine Cotton at thirty-three to one.
Most bookies put up seven to two. Punters hurl abuse
as they sprint up and down the line, trying to get set
before every bookie has turned the price in. Next call
it's eight to one; bookies working the race go odds on,
and stay there when the call before they jump has it at
seven to two. The favourite's price has blown all the way
out to the Black Stump.

Of course the horse sprints out of the field after the jump
and chases down the favourite. He hardly crosses the line
when a roar goes up, on every race track in the country so
I'm told, and as far away as betting shops in Darwin, and
Fiji, of Ring-In! Ring-In! about the worst-kept secret
in the racing world ever. The punters abuse The Boss
as if he's part of it. He laughs, but his eyes turn very
black.

Turns out some in his family are warned off race-tracks
all over the country for this, and lose their licences too.

The mysterious 'they' plan for a long time to win this race
with a ring-in for Fine Cotton; they buy a horse, almost
identical colour and markings, and set everything up.
Before the race their ring-in is injured, no way can it win.
The word's already out, there's some large investments
made by some hard people who will be very angry. 'They'
panic a bit, send for a new horse, buy Bold Personality,
not cheap but he can definitely win the race. Wrong
colour? A few bottles of Lady Clairol
turns bay into brown, though bleach
on his hind legs to make white patches
doesn't work. By now, hours before starting time,
they're convinced they have no choice, and open
that can of white paint.

Seems odd to me, very unsophisticated for this family.
Who paints a horse? It goes to weigh-in dripping paint.
Even Eagle Farm stewards have to take some action.
They tell bookies not to pay out on the race. There's
a riot brewing. Everyone knows the real story, and
they're all different.

The contrast in time sticks in my mind. Ninety seconds
of race time, then decades of court cases, wasted lives,
ruined careers, marriages, other relationships as well.
I can't decide if it's just cheeky, Aussie larrikin style,
or if it's really cheating. Whether Father O'Dwyer,
for example, would call it a sin.

The SP joint

The Boss sacks me, a shock because I don't do anything wrong. Mr. Nasty's brother Bluey says it's a warning to Mr. Nasty. I cop it sweet and look for another job, get asked if I want to work for an SP.

I ask George his opinion. George is another penciler. He once ran Sydney's biggest Two Up game. He never says much, but it's always worth hearing. 'Ron' he says. 'Used to run a casino, classy joint, made a lot of money out of Yanks on R & R' which is as close to a reference as I'm going to get. I ask others. Everyone knows Ron.

The buzz says he's partnered up with an actor's agent who owns a few racehorses, and the brother of a trainer of two-year-olds, who works for the stable as manager. Ron gets the drum on which runner has been kept overnight in the dungeon. I think Ron runs the operation, the manager provides information and stable gossip, and the agent puts up the cash.

We meet in a café in Double Bay and get on OK.
The job's for Saturday gallops, answering phones
and taking down bets. Next, an interview with the agent
to stars. He welcomes me, asks me to let him know
if Ron or the other clerks do anything suss. I don't
get to meet the stable manager. He doesn't want his
involvement known, though it seems a public secret.

Next Saturday I arrive at the address, second story
above a hairdresser in New South Head Road,
an accountant's office. He has the disease too,
is into Ron for heaps, and happy to do a favour
by lending his office on Saturday afternoons.
'We move around a bit' says Ron. 'Makes it harder
for the cops to track me.' Like it's a game they play.

Ron has a phone tech in his kick, who sets him up
a system he can use anywhere there's a phone plug.
It's hard to trace. It holds his speed dials for certain
numbers, punters' contacts, a kill switch that wipes
everything instantly, if he gets busted.

He has two other clerks, one his girlfriend of decades.
She'd marry him like a shot she says but his Catholic wife
won't consider divorce. I think she's warning me off.
The other clerk, Ron's 2IC, is a guy
ten years older than me; he keeps track
of who's backing what, and Ron lays off
when he thinks they hold too much.
It's fast-paced for five minutes,
three times an hour. Between races
we drink coffee and chat. Well paid,
cash in hand after the last race.
Three weeks go by. We get raided.

As the door slams open Ron hits the kill switch. I'm out
through the window beside me without thinking about it.
Belinda follows me but we're ten feet
above the pavement, is it worth breaking
a leg? Cops jump through the window
and grab us, take us to the police station
in Waverley. We're charged with using
a premises for illegal off-course betting,
held until Ron's lawyer arrives. We sign
bail undertakings, Ron hands us our pay,
with a bit extra 'for all the fuss'. He'll pay
any fine, which won't be much, it's only
a misdemeanor. Ron tells me not to worry,
I can be busted a hundred times, the penalty
will never be more than a small fine. Until
the law changes. Licensed or unlicensed,
the work is the same.
This fuss feels like much ado about nothing.

I go to Court, and get busted again

I turn up early, with time to read the boards and find my name on the court list. According to this list, I'm charged with being present on a premises being used for prostitution. I spin out. Not likely my grandmother who lives in Traralgon will see this, but even so. I make a fuss. Someone has typed automatically a more usual charge than SP betting. I wonder about the difference.

Both illegal, both victimless crimes, so why do I feel prostitution is worse? I'm being a hypocrite, I realize, as I find the right court. Ron has paid a QC to represent us all, which feels like a bit of overkill, but he's paying, so it's his choice. This silk usually engages with complex and scandalous criminal cases. This must be like a holiday to him.

Full courtroom, I can hear
only mumbles from the bench. Then it's over,
I'm guilty, we're all guilty. Ron grins, takes care
of it all. Gives me a card, construction company,
with an address pencilled on the back. 'Keep it
to yourself. See you Saturday.'

An architect's office, this time, ground floor of a high-rise
right next to the new Police Centre under construction.
Cheeky, I think, but Ron knows what he's doing, it's his
career and he's a professional. We spread out, set up,
and the calls start coming in. I recognize
a lot of the voices now, know whose bet
is the drum when it sets Ron dialling.

A woman's voice sends shivers down my spine each time.
'Norma Lee' she announces, no greeting, just her name,
then the bet. No one wants to talk about her so I figure
she's from the underworld, another strata of society
interpenetrating the worlds of races, and of the straights,
the police, and the politicians, goes beyond them even.
I don't need to know who or how.

And it happens again – working flat out on the first leg of the Melbourne daily double when the locked doors burst open and in come the cops. This time we're taken to Sydney Central, fingerprinted, photographed, I'm left alone in a dark dirty cell this time, kept there for hours. Not so exciting. And I'm sure I've seen the head of one of the arresting cops. Not in uniform, either.

Court case is a ditto of the first. I stare at the cop, and Bingo! There it is! An image of the cop, at the trots last Friday night, Harold Park, talking to the phone tech who fixes Ron's phone system. I think he's stitched Ron right up, working for both sides. It's none of my business.

I want to tell Ron he's been set up, but I don't tell him his partner asks me to spy on him, so why change now? In the end I tell him about both.

Ron rings me the next week. A few things have changed, he's working for himself again, do I want to work next Saturday? I'll be on my own, just answering the phone.

The address is a bedsit unit in Randwick, obviously home to a woman. The decor shrieks baby pink from walls, cushions, lights. There's a balcony overlooking a tropical garden, with an almost life-sized statue, vaguely Grecian, taking up half of it. The toilet has a fluffy pink cover. It matches the bath mat, shower curtains, towels, and the crocheted doll's dress that covers a spare toilet paper roll. The wall and floor tiles are lime green. Disturbing.

I get two phone calls a race, max, all for pocket money. I wander uneasily through the unit. Ron tells me to help myself to coffee, anything in the fridge I like, but I feel like a trespasser, in a way that I didn't in the offices we occupied. This is more intimate, makes me feel dirty. I'm having enough problems with self-esteem at the moment. When Ron collects the paperwork, I say I can't work for him any more. He thanks me, says he's disappointed, get in touch if ever I need anything, but I never actually see him again.

Frank Hardy

I'm a fan of his writing since first I read 'Power without Glory', think about going to readings he gives at Wentworth Park Hotel, monthly, but I never make it. Mr. Nasty never reads a novel in his life. He says he's dyslexic. He doesn't read anything except the board on the stand, but mentions to The Boss I have Hardy's books at home so The Boss next Saturday at Randwick introduces me to his new nod punter. Frank's happy to chat about his work, surprised that a bookie's clerk reads.

Next week he turns up at Rosehill with a copy of his latest book, 'Who shot George Kirkland' which he inscribes to me, with best wishes. George Kirkland is a character in 'Power'. I wonder who the actual person is. Identities of leading characters are obvious to anyone with knowledge of the local scene.

No publisher wants to touch his first book. Hardy
self-publishes, sets off legal cases, has all copies of
the book confiscated by a court. Being a Communist
doesn't help.

The people of his books, the SP betting, construction
companies, influence of politics and Church, unions,
stand-over men, police and lawyers of Melbourne,
all have their counterparts here at the Sydney tracks.

I want to ask Frank about George Kirkland, but Frank
vanishes from the races. Apparently he's gone back
to Melbourne, owing a fortune to the Sydney bookies
who extended him credit. Like a wave he came in,
and went, leaving the ocean undiminished.

My Irish Setter pup loses her milk teeth in the cover
of 'George Kirkland', chewing it beyond repair. 'Gone
to the dogs' I think. 'Gone to Gowings.' I don't
throw the book away for a decade though, until
after I hear of Frank's death.

The moneybox

Harold Park after Randwick. A good crowd tonight, even the away ring looks busy, but Mr. Nasty's under strict instructions to limit payouts, to turn the price off and stay under the odds once he's laid the favourite.

No excitement, no backing back, it's all a bit boring. Something's going on in the local ring though, a bunch of punters whistling and clapping. Mr. Nasty sprints off to suss out what's happening. I follow.

People in a ring around a bookie's stand. In the middle a young couple collects big fists of cash. Punters cheer and whistle, abusing the bookie with their usual calls.

The bloke stuffs his pockets full, jacket and pants;
the girl's handbag bulges, about to burst. They're
both laughing, you can feel the excitement, punters
sharing their magic of winning, waiting for their turn
to dance with Lady Luck, never doubting that one day
it will come.

'They won big at Randwick today' Mr. Nasty remembers
seeing them in the Member's 'and they've doubled it
here tonight. No idea what they're backing, pick a name
or a number they like, and they just can't go wrong.'

'Never been to the races before,' someone says, 'never
even had a bet.' George frowns, taps his glasses.
'Worst thing that can happen to anyone, winning
their first bet.'

The couple wanders up to the away ring, bet with Roger,
who winces. Now they have a problem, where to put
the cash? The girl stuffs bundles of notes into her bra
'til it's full, but there's still more money to put away.

Everyone watches as she grabs the hem of her skirt,
raises it, and shoves a wad of cash into the waist
of her pantyhose; a quick flash of plump thighs,
lacey petticoat and knickers, and she drops the hem.
The ring erupts into cheers, whistles, cat-calls, laughter.

'She's putting it in her moneybox!' yells Blue.

Everyone cracks up, all over again.
Mr. Nasty is still cruising mellow
as we reach the alley where Old Tom
parks cars, keeps a eye on them.
We're just in time to watch a stranger
drive our car away. 'He said
you wanted him to pick you up.
Called you Mr. Nasty so I figured
he was on the level.'

No tip for Old Tom this week. Mr. Nasty growls.

'Lucky the house key isn't on that ring.'
I attempt to deflect tension.

'Don't talk to me about luck! I'm fucking sick of
fucking luck!'

Dead silence.

The wong Wong

Sidney Wong, one of our nod punters, owns Chinatown.
We eat at his Old Tai Pei sometimes between meetings,
a dozen or so clerks who have to be at work in an hour.
We're in and out, no muss, no fuss, and they can reset
the tables before dinner starts pumping. They like that.

Henry claims us for his section. He's worked there
forever, gets the best tables. 'Ya, ya, I fix for you,
I fix for you' the only English he speaks. He knows
what we want for starters (dim sum and gow ghee,
steamed and deep fried, soy and chili sauces to mix),
what beer to bring, (Crown Lager), darts into the steam,
screaming what could be curses or orders, earns
the good tip we leave.

One night Henry doesn't get a tip. Sidney's new horse
wins that day. (He bets with us, but not on the locals.)
He celebrates, sends champagne, insists on paying
for our meal, won't let us even leave a tip. Poor Henry.
I hope he backed it.

Sidney's son Robert, who runs the family restaurants with
sister Deena, punts with us too. I know his head
from the track, a tall, good-looking dude, always polite.
The heavies show him a lot of respect. Never meet Deena,
just see her head in the kitchen, but I hear stories.

Two Wongs in the nod book gets confusing.
Marvin the Prawn has instructions to ring
Robert's bets so they stand out, but he gets
them mixed up. Seems that's lucky for The Boss
though. He keeps leaning over Marvin all day, saying
'Make sure – don't wing the wong Wong' and cracking up.
Marvin's face stays bright red.

I think of Marvin when Sidney is murdered in bed,
his wife asleep beside him. Deena, charged with
importing heroin, collapses in a Sydney court
as she's about to give evidence, dies
without regaining consciousness.

Seems Robert is the right Wong after all.

Messing about in boats

When I decide not to go back to the States, Mr. Nasty
decides it would be nice to buy a yacht, learn to sail,
and head off into the sunset; at least, Great Barrier Reef.
Each week we visit a different broker, checking out boats.

I'm not working, Mr. Nasty has good cash flow,
no savings, limiting what we can borrow.
We look bargain basement, find a concrete-hull
in a Middle Harbour marina, maybe something
we can work on and the price is right. We pay
for hauling it out of the water, crane fees, yard
and slip fees, etc. We ring a marine engineer
to assess it for us. He wants the hull clean
before he'll look. It takes us days of slog
to scrape off years of accumulated
barnacles and weed.
The hull is cracked.

So we already learn how yachts are holes in the water
where you pour money. A broker calls: he's found
a 32' multi-chine steel hull cutter rigged bilge keeler,
self-steering gear, only two years old. The seller builds it
himself, sails with his wife and baby from Brisbane
up to Lizard Island and back. Takes a year for the trip,
pays for his diesel by selling frozen fillets of reef fish
to the marinas where he puts in for fuel and water.
Now he wants to take the family back to New Guinea,
so Tapini is for sale.

We see some photos. Mr. Nasty pays a deposit, negotiates
the price down by 20%, delivery to Palm Beach included.
All we have to do is find the rest of the money. We start
with Mr. Nasty's bank. They're happy to lend him half.

My half isn't so easy; not working,
just back in the country, no bank account.
Mr. Nasty meets his loan manager again,
who grants me a personal loan; Tapini
is ours. We meet her
at the Palm Beach Marina a week later, moor her there
just down the hill from the Tower. Now to learn to sail.

Mr. Nasty has problems with 'port' and 'starboard',
gets the boat rerigged colour-coded so he can yell
'Pull on the red rope!' or 'Pull on the blue rope!'
until he works it out.

Pittwater's a great learner's pool. We make progress
but it's not all forward. We snap the mast one day when
Mr. Nasty is trying to get one of the keels
to break surface, like he sees
the Hobie Cats do all around us. As we heel
right over, a gust – I can see it rushing toward us, water
darkening in wrinkles – hits. A stay snaps, shrouds go
whizzing like blades around us, the mast breaks, sails
flap and settle over us, over the deck.

Lucky the bank insists on insurance. We're sailing again
in a month. We spend all our spare time
on her, learn how the diesel engine works,
how to fix the small pump toilet.
After one hung-over opening of the freezer and a quick
feeding of fish over the side, we learn to empty it before
we disembark.

We're asleep at the mooring one dawn,
when the marina guy bangs on the hull.
'Message for Mr. Nasty: get home quick'.
I stay aboard with his two half-brothers.
They won't wake up for hours yet,
exhausted by yesterday's sailing and swimming.
Peter the houseboy sends the message.
Mr. Nasty finds the Tower full of cops who
want to arrest him. They haven't found
what they came looking for, though they've
pretty well torn the house apart. They find
our bong, a long bamboo pipe. Mr. Nasty
apologizes that he can't pack them a cone,
we finished the stick yesterday, shows them
dust in the mull bowl. No one wants to carry
the bong, they say it stinks, so they leave it.

They think he owns the Tower.
He shows them rent receipts.
Doesn't own the new car, it comes
with his job. Shows them loan documents
for Tapini, explains how he wins the jet boat
from a punter at the track. They ask why
he needs a telescope. He tells them
he wins it in a card game. They ask
for a few thousand good reasons why
they shouldn't run him in. He tells them
he has only a few hundred. This is definitely
not what the cops expect. They chat
amongst themselves again, ring the station.
Mr. Nasty overhears one say 'Only a small fry'.
He watches one of them take plastic baggies
of white powder from our flour container.
They leave with a promise they can still come back.

We soon find out what it's all about, through
a contact at Manly Police. A Supreme Court Judge,
just retired, buys a house down the hill from us.
He sees us in the village, at the Tower, sees us
in a new car, on two boats, knows we work
at the races. Mr. Nasty abuses everyone
in the Members stand at racetracks as a matter
of course. They're dirty politicians and judges,
lawyers and bankers; scum of the earth
he calls them, laughs as he does it.
No one's ever spoken to this judge that way.
He doesn't like it.

The judge gets tired and emotional one night
with his mate Johnny Walker, sees us lighting
fireworks from the Tower, just having fun,
decides we're signalling ships at sea
so they can drop drugs tied to a buoy.
We collect them in our boats and sell them,
he decides, rings his mate in Manly Police,
who sets up a raid.

Lucky the police don't bother checking out Tapini,
I say, and we don't lose these temple balls
of sweet Nepalese hash. Lucky I don't have
to throw them overboard. 'Mate' says Mr. Nasty,
'mate, I was shitting myself' and he takes
another good deep toke.

Superstitions

Every punter believes in a supernatural power.
They each have a charm, token, totem, fetish,
prayer, chant, or secret ritual process, to invoke
Lady Luck.

For The Teacher, it's the number of consonants
the same, in the name. Doesn't matter if it's a dog,
trotter, flats galloper or steeplechaser, if it has three
letters the same, he backs it.

For others, it's the numbers, or strange combinations
of them: wins, places, barrier draws, weights carried.

Old Jim, the Boss's father, is highly allergic to the colour
green. He expects his staff to know this. If they turn up
for work wearing anything green he sends them home,
no pay for the day. Taking off the green item isn't enough.

He won't change his clothes, either. If he comes to work
wearing an overcoat, he won't take it off,
even when the day warms up. Won't even
put on a coat when it rains. He thinks
changing clothes will change his luck.

So does putting up an umbrella to shelter his workers.
He says it hides his name. You have to tell him the book
is too wet to write in, before he relents. 'This is only
a light shower' he says, while lightning and thunder play.
'It will clear up in a minute'.

He suffers on autumn afternoons after rain,
when the sky clears and heat builds up. He stands
in his hat, full three-piece suit, and heavy overcoat,
while sweat pours down his face. Punters in shirt-sleeves
make fun of him. He ignores them, endures in silence,
but takes grim satisfaction in watching punters rush
for the train after the meeting.

'You can tell who's winning' he says to me one day
in the Rosehill carpark, leaning out the window of his
Rolls-Royce. 'Just from the way we get here'.

Some jockeys are deadly

We're sitting with Robbie, Mr. Nasty's father
in his house on The Tor Walk, Castlecrag, watching
tour boats cruise by below, the guide's voice clear
as he describes this suburb built by Walter Burley Griffin,
the architect who went on to design
and set out the nation's new capital,
Canberra, in a sheep paddock halfway
between Melbourne and Sydney.

'I fielded in Canberra a few times
in the seventies' says Robbie.
'Did my money.'

'Is that why you give up the races,'
I ask, 'build things instead?'

He's happy to talk, chatty, now the pain
from his lung cancer is finally under control.

'I know why you take those drugs, son'
he says to Mr. Nasty. 'I went to Paris last night.'

To me 'I give up the races when I almost get killed
one night. Lose interest after that.' As you would,
I think.

He describes how he gets to his car
in the carpark after winning just enough
for the rent, throws the bag in the back,
gets in, winds down the window, puts the key
in the ignition, about to start up when
something hard and cold presses
against his right temple.

'My balls tuck straight back up into my gut.' Remembered
terror etches his face. 'I know it's a gun. Then the voice
Get over. Now! Jockey Smith. I know him, he's dead set
Yarra, meaner than a cut snake. He holds up two bookies
already, shoots them, kills Lloyd Tidmarsh. I scramble
over the T Bar and handbrake, not easy for me, a tubby.
He gets in the driver's seat.

Don't look at me, cunt. Put your head down. He's going to drive me somewhere to kill me. That's what he does with the others. I tell him he can have my money, it's in the bag in the back, I haven't won much, but it's his.

I grovel. I piss myself. I stare at my boots, wondering if I'll see my kids again, how Mary will manage without me.

The Jockey's nervous, jittery, fumbles with his gun, drops the key, curses, picks it up, jams it in, and the car won't start. He tries again. He's getting anxious, I can hear it in his voice. I've never before been so glad to be driving a heap of shit. He won't shoot me here, too many people around, too hard to get away.
He curses some more, grabs the cash
from the bag, tells me to keep my head
down, don't move until I count to 100,
very slowly.

My mate's in a car over there he says *with a rifle.*
He'll shoot if you try anything clever
and he's gone.

I keep my head down for a very long time, just in case.

I'm a coward, yes, but you'd be a fool not to be a coward
when some nutter's got a gun pointed at you. That's it,
for me. I never field at a track again.'

His youngest son rushes in, to demonstrate the new steps
he's learned in his tap dancing lesson.
Robbie winks at me over his head.
'This is worth more than all the money
at all the tracks in the world, love.
Sure, there are bludgers everywhere,
but I figure the odds this way: I'm less likely
to get shot over a building extension,
or a deck, than I am for cash I don't even have.
I figure my life is worth more than
a couple of hundred bucks.'

The ashes

Robbie leaves instructions. He wants
to be cremated, his ashes scattered
into Sydney Harbour near North Head
while the tide's going out. He wants to be
part of the Pacific Ocean.

Six months after the funeral, Mr. Nasty
books a cruiser from a Cremorne marina
and we work out the best time and place to
catch the outgoing tide, send him off
as he wanted.

We round up the mourners and meet
at the marina; about a dozen of us:
the widow, two of his sons, a couple
of clerks who once worked for him,
a couple each of bookies, builders,
neighbours, and friends.

Mr. Nasty's brother Blue takes over
the job of captain, steers us in the right
direction. We make a mistake about tides
though so we have to wait, floating on
gentle swells under the hot sun, harbour
busy with boats all around us, telling tales
of Robbie at home, at the races, and
drinking wine. Everyone becomes tired
and emotional. The widow weeps openly
as we drift near North Head.

When we all agree the tide has turned,
definitely, Blue brings out the plastic urn
provided by the crematorium, ready to
open and shake, but it's sealed, there's
no way to open it except with a blade.
Which no-one has.

The only implement of any kind we find
on board is a corkscrew. The widow won't
let us throw the urn in the water to bob.
Blue takes charge, stabbing holes in the urn
with the corkscrew, again and again, tiny
holes that no ashes can come out of.
The widow is very disturbed by the stabbing,
weeps some more.

'Don't worry, love, can't hurt him now'
comforts Mr. Nasty, but that doesn't help.

Blue stabs his own hand, hard. 'Ah fuck this!'
he throws the holey urn into the harbour,
turns the boat around, and heads us towards
the dock. The widow wails 'I can still see it!
It's bobbing!'

Blue convinces her that water will seep in
soon, the urn will sink, Robbie's ashes will
mingle with the ocean in no time at all.

We disembark, after a slight altercation with
the edge of the dock, and go our different ways,
happy that Robbie's wishes are carried out. Now
there's some closure.

Six weeks later the crematorium contacts us.
Someone up the coast in Gosford picks up the urn
on the beach, tracks down where it comes from,
worried someone has lost it. Can we come and
collect it again please.

This time we make no fuss. We bury the balance
under a bush in the Tower garden at Palm Beach.
Mr. Nasty says there's enough of his ashes dissolved
in the ocean between North Head and Gosford
to say his wishes are carried out. No one's game
to get the widow weeping again.

About the Author

Mercedes Webb-Pullman comes from Kaitaia, Far North New Zealand. She sailed off for her Overseas Experience in 1969, lived in Australia and California, and finally returned in 2008.

She's worked in diverse places, doing interesting things, from mobile ski repairs to horse trekking, from bookmaker's clerk to Trust Account bookkeeping, from cocktail bars to hotel management. Since completing her MA in 2010 she now writes about them. Her work has been published worldwide.

Her books include *Tasseography, Looking for Kerouac, Collected poems 2008 – 2014, After the Danse, Ono, Bravo Charlie Foxtrot, Numeralla Dreaming, Food 4 Thought*. All are available in print, or Kindle from Amazon.

Acknowledgements

'A fair dinkum champion' was previously published in *True Truth Serum Vol. 1* (Truth Serum Press)

'Not-So-Fine Cotton was previously published in *Wiser Truth Serum Vol. 2* (Truth Serum Press)

'A giant walnut' was previously published in *UMPh Prose Issue 5*

From Everytime Press
http://www.everytimepress.com/apps/webstore/

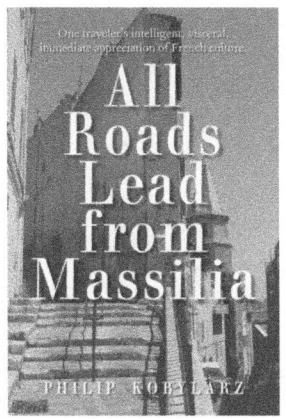

All Roads Lead from Massilia
978-1-925536-27-0 (paperback)
978-1-925536-28-7 (eBook)

Kobylarz's reflections on terraces, baked delicacies, Cézanne, the essence of walls, the erotic life, poverty and Super Gluing one's shoes, French doors, the hazards of solitude, café contemplation, hiking, the birth echo of caves with "crystals like immediate stars," leave the reader with the overall absorbed sensuality and meteorology of the landscape remaining, against most odds, among the lasting values of a sane, enthusiastic, contemplative life-affirming sensibility.

Also from Truth Serum Press
http://truthserumpress.net/catalogue/

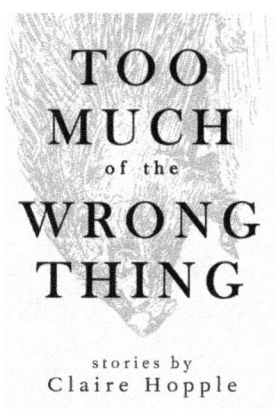

Too Much of the Wrong Thing
978-1-925536-33-1 (paperback)
978-1-925536-34-8 (eBook)

At first glance Claire Hopple's stories appear delightfully off kilter, even laugh-out-loud funny, but the flashes of wisdom start early in this collection and they don't stop. This is a world of constant disorientation where people aim for connection and gamble on intimacy, no matter how precarious. After watching Hopple's characters question the scripts they've been handed, we are left to marvel at the hard work of being lost.

Also from Truth Serum Press
http://truthserumpress.net/catalogue/

Wiser Truth Serum Vol. #2
978-1-925536-31-7 (paperback)
978-1-925536-32-4 (eBook)

Stories, essays and poetry by Alex Reece Abbott, Duff Allen, Paul Beckman, Claudia Bierschenk, Rick Blum, Irene Buckler, Ron Campbell, Steven Carr, Jan Chronister, Ruth Z. Deming, Matt Dennison, Nod Ghosh, Jack Granath, John Grey, Louise Hofmeister, Mark Hudson, Len Kuntz, John Lambremont, Sr., Larry Lefkowitz, Cynthia Leslie-Bole, Michael Marrotti, Todd McKie, Lesley Middleton, Gwendolyn Joyce Mintz, Piet Nieuwland, Martin Jon Porter, Stephen V. Ramey, Alex Robertson, Ruth Sabath Rosenthal, Wayne Scheer, Martin Shaw, DL Shirey, Jan Elman Stout, Sophie Van Llewyn, Jerry Vilhotti, Rob Walker, Mercedes Webb-Pullman and Allan J. Wills

Also from Truth Serum Press
http://truthserumpress.net/catalogue/

True Truth Serum Vol. #1
978-1-925536-29-4 (paperback)
978-1-925536-30-0 (eBook)

Stories, essays and poetry by Mercedes Webb-Pullman, Mark Hudson, Lynn Hoffman, Len Kuntz, Danielle Davis, M. Earl Smith, Wayne Scheer, Sally Reno, Vivian Wagner, Paul Beckman, Michael Konik, David S. Atkinson, A J Huffman, Jack Granath, Tim Philippart, Martin Jon Porter, Martin Shaw, Sylvia Aguilar-Zéleny, Ruth Z. Deming, John Lambremont Sr., John Grey, Em König, Brian Abiri-Osare, Patricia Walsh, Samuel Cole, Danny P. Barbare, Carl 'Papa' Palmer, Michael Marrotti, Barbara Ruth, Stephen V. Ramey, Ruth Sabath Rosenthal, Irene Buckler, Robbi Nester, Flora Gaugg, Matt Devirgiliis, Sarah Anne Childers, Robert Beveridge, Anne E. Weisgerber, Richard King Perkins II, Nod Ghosh, Alan Walowitz, Tom Sheehan, Dusty-Anne Rhodes, Lynn White and Gwendolyn Joyce Mintz

Also from Truth Serum Press
http://truthserumpress.net/catalogue/

happyme@t.us
978-1-925536-07-2 (paperback)
978-1-925536-08-9 (eBook)

To be everywhere and nowhere, all at once … Through her stories, Kim Conklin takes us on a journey of the human condition, where the everyday becomes foreign and dangerous, while the oddities of our world provide us with strange comfort. Each story is unsettling, passionate, thoughtful, provocative and reaffirming; taking the reader everywhere and nowhere, all at once. Dark tales, deftly told.

Also from Truth Serum Press
http://truthserumpress.net/catalogue/

Luck and Other Truths
978-1-925101-77-5 (paperback)
978-1-925536-04-1 (eBook)

Richard Mark Glover spins larger-than-life tales of folks on the fringe in places where they tend to collect, with the focus on that great empty space known as Far West Texas. What might appear to outsiders as a whole bunch of harsh forbidding nothing – think Cormac McCarthy – these stories are filled with quirky characters brought to life by Glover's observant eye and quirk-spotting pen.

Also from Truth Serum Press
http://truthserumpress.net/catalogue/

Hello Berlin!
978-1-925536-11-9 (paperback)
978-1-925536-12-6 (eBook)

Paul is an average Joe from London. He arrives in Berlin during the exciting noughties and discovers a world of free love, free afternoons and lofty literary pursuits. Clueless and curiously innocent, Paul steals the hearts of those around him, leading to anything but a tender love story. Fresh and honest.

Also from Truth Serum Press
http://truthserumpress.net/catalogue/

Deer Michigan
978-1-925536-25-6 (paperback)
978-1-925536-26-3 (eBook)

"Something quite wonderful happens when you allow yourself to drift through life without a plan of direction," writes Jack C. Buck. *Deer Michigan* takes this heart, embracing the flux of fate in over fifty ethereal narratives. In one story we meet an exiled Mao on a hiking trail, in another the narrator mourns the graceful disappearance of birds. Buck's stories ripple with nostalgia, a reverence for the natural world and an America with room in which to wander. Though the stories in *Deer Michigan* are short, they bottle up an expanse of human experience, offering a stunning universe of feeling.

Also from Truth Serum Press
http://truthserumpress.net/catalogue/

What Came Before
978-1-925536-05-8 (paperback)
978-1-925536-06-5 (eBook)

Five words scribbled on a discarded piece of paper ignite old memories for Abbie Palmer and lead to the explosive uncovering of a fifty-year-old mystery. *What Came Before* rumbles along at break-neck speed. The quirky characters and tightly-written plots of Ms. Degani's short stories have long been enjoyable and her novel doesn't disappoint either. The book presents great characters, including a strong older-female protagonist, and ably-managed twists and turns through the streets and people of modern-day Los Angeles, as well as the L.A. of 50 years ago. Old-school suspense at its best.

Also from Truth Serum Press
http://truthserumpress.net/catalogue/

Rain Check
978-1-925536-09-6 (paperback)
978-1-925536-10-2 (eBook)

Beautifully rendered, the stories in *Rain Check* could well be the footprints and photographs of our own lives if we'd have taken risks as daring as Noe's characters. Each misstep, triumph and regret rings true. Reading these stories is like being a lucky voyeur who happens upon an artist with brush in hand, nearing the finishing touch of their masterpiece. Nothing is more potent than prose that lifts off the page and lands, like a well-placed bullet or caress, on the heart, and that's precisely what Noe has done here.

Also from Truth Serum Press
http://truthserumpress.net/catalogue/

Based on True Stories
978-1-925101-75-1 (paperback)
978-1-925101-76-8 (eBook)

The small fictions in *Based on True Stories* will not lull you – they will piss you off or, at the least, move you to indignation, or tears, or laughter. Maybe all three. These gems provoke, like the tip of a chef's knife pricking skin, and just as the words get uncomfortable, the story delivers the bit of redemption that reveals the humanity of his characters – and of us all. These stories are real, raw, and honest. The reading doesn't get much better than that.

Also from Truth Serum Press
http://truthserumpress.net/catalogue/

La Ronde
978-1-925101-64-5 (paperback)
978-1-925101-65-2 (eBook)

Try putting *La Ronde* down after you've begun to read – not possible. It sweeps you up into a beguiling tale of greed, mistaken identity, and desire. Townsend Walker has crafted a chilling novella with characters that pop off the page and events that will make you squirm ... a tale of greed and desire that will make you wonder ... what would your spouse do if he or she wanted to kill you?

Also from Truth Serum Press
http://truthserumpress.net/catalogue/

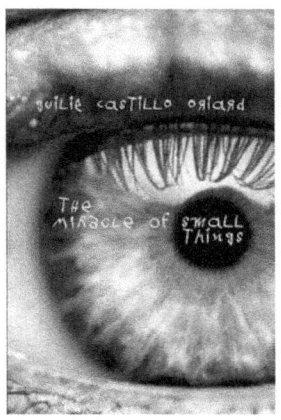

The Miracle of Small Things

978-1-925101-73-7 (paperback)
978-1-925101-74-4 (eBook)

The Miracle of Small Things beguiles the reader with a witty and compassionate portrait of a year in the life of Luis Villalobos in tropical Curaçao, where nothing is quite what it seems, and all can be lost or gained in a summer afternoon on the beach. Told deftly, with humor and insight into our very human vulnerabilities, this lovely novella by Guilie Castillo Oriard builds upon that quest for happiness we share, a sense of belonging, and makes us want to travel south to find our own miracle.

From Pure Slush Books
http://pureslush.webs.com/store.htm

The Company of Men
978-1-925101-06-5 (paperback)
978-1-925101-10-2 (Kindle eBook)
978-1-925101-09-6 (ePub eBook)

With the clarity of the child's eye and the wisdom of the adult's hindsight seamlessly working together in the writer's voice, Brenta effortlessly reels the reader into her charming fictional memoir. While all the family members – as well as the servants who tend them – are deftly drawn, the conservative and indomitable grandmother is the pivotal character. Her slow but astonishing transformation teaches the young girl timeless lessons about class and power and love. If you know and adore Italy even a little bit, you will fall under the languid and colorful spell of *The Company of Men*. Bellissimo.

www.ingramcontent.com/pod-product-compliance
Lightning Source LLC
Chambersburg PA
CBHW051808040426
42446CB00007B/577